Original title:

Under the Warmth of the Sun

Copyright © 2025 Creative Arts Management OÜ
All rights reserved.

Author: Liam Sterling
ISBN HARDBACK: 978-1-80581-583-9
ISBN PAPERBACK: 978-1-80581-110-7
ISBN EBOOK: 978-1-80581-583-9

Harmony in the Radiance

Bumblebees buzzing, oh what a sound,
Tickled by petals, they dance all around.
Sunglasses perched on a daisy so bright,
Sharing gossip with clouds in pure flight.

Chasing their shadows, the squirrels run fast,
Collecting the acorns, oh, what a blast!
The sun's golden giggle spills over the land,
While butterflies organize a conga band.

The Promise of a New Dawn

Roosters are crowing, it's time to get up,
Coffee in one hand, the other a cup.
The toast pops up, it's a glorious sight,
Dancing with jelly, a breakfast delight.

The cat tries to catch the beam of the morn,
But falls on the floor, with a chair nearly torn.
With laughter erupting, we start our new day,
Silly moments scattered like breadcrumbs of play.

A Symphony of Brightness

The sun plays the trumpet, the trees gently sway,
Birds join in harmony, all wanting to play.
A frog sings a solo from the edge of the creek,
While ants throw a party, no room for the meek.

Sunbathers on towels, catching rays with delight,
While a dog in the sand is a comical sight.
With splashes and laughter, our worries all flee,
As the warmth on our backs feels like life's recipe.

Awakening to the Light

Pancakes stack high, with syrup like gold,
Giggles and chatter, the stories unfold.
Sun hats on ducks as they waddle along,
Quacking a tune—they've got rhythm, so strong!

The lawnmower roars, it's a wild serenade,
Neighbors compete for who'll make the best shade.
As we dance through the day, with laughter and cheer,
It's clear we could party with sunlight all year.

The Radiant Sky's Serenade

Up on the roof, I stretch and yawning,
The cat's sunbathing; it's up to no good.
Neighbors wave while their gardens are fawning,
I'm here with my snack, feeling quite understood.

Birds sing a tune, but I sing along wrong,
A dance with my sandwich, a waltz that's quite airy.
The mailbox has moved, oh where does it belong?
This sky's a big joke, and I'm just the dairy.

Harvesting Day's Brilliance

Corn in the field, golden as cheese,
I tiptoe through rows like a cow on parade.
With butter and popcorn, I'm aiming to please,
But bees circle round like they've come for a trade.

The farmer's hat, it flaps with delight,
While I eye the tomatoes, all plump and so red.
One jumped off the vine, like a thief in the night,
Waving goodbye as I flee with my bread.

Where Shadows Play in Light

With my trusty friend, we chase after flies,
Our shadows stretch long, like spaghetti on plates.
We laugh and we tumble, oh what a surprise,
A game of tag where no one waits.

The sun sneaks in, making figures of fun,
We dance with the trees, like we're fetching a prize.
The squirrels roll their eyes, in this brightened run,
As we race through the grass, much to their surprise.

Sun-Drenched Memories

Picnics with sandwiches, daring the ants,
Bestowing my secrets to clouds up above.
With ice cream drips landing like odd little plants,
I giggle at moments I cherish with love.

The sun-hat brigade, we march side by side,
Waving bright colors, we're goofy and free.
In this hot cabinet of laughter, our pride,
We'll fret not at life, just sip lemonade tea.

The Dance of Light and Life

Bumblebees buzz in a wobbly line,
Dancing round flowers, sipping sweet wine.
The sun's like a spotlight, we take our cues,
Even the daisies are sporting bright hues.

Grasshoppers leap with jiggly surprise,
Chasing the shadows that flicker and rise.
A squirrel does twirls, and oh, what a sight!
All creatures are waltzing, feeling just right.

Sunkissed Meadows Calling

In meadows so bright, the daisies play tricks,
They hide from the shadows, poke fun at our picks.
The sun makes us squint, a bright ball of cheer,
While we trip over paths, and let out a cheer.

Caterpillars croon a soft, silly song,
While butterflies giggle, drifting along.
Each clover, a dancer, with roots stuck in ground,
Only the clouds seem to frown all around.

Joy Beneath a Burning Sky

Children are painting the world with pure glee,
Splashing bright colors like birds on a spree.
The sun steals the show, a comedian bright,
Joking with shadows that wobble in light.

Picnics erupt with sandwiches flying,
Ants march in formation, oh how they're trying!
Lemons act sour, but we laugh along,
Joy's the sweet chorus and nature's our song.

Illuminated Paths Ahead

With sun on our backs, we travel, we roam,
Seeking adventure wherever we comb.
A dog with a hat thinks he's quite the dude,
While squirrels critique him, oh, that's so rude!

The path is a dance floor for critters of all,
Bouncing and prancing, they're having a ball.
We join in the fun as the daylight grows long,
With laughter and joy, we can do no wrong.

Joyous Echoes of the Earth

In fields of laughter, flowers bloom,
Bees dance a jig, dispel the gloom.
A squirrel in shades, a nutty spree,
Chasing its tail, how silly can we be?

The grass wears green like a vibrant dress,
As birds start gossiping, what a mess!
A rabbit hops in shades of gray,
Chasing its shadow, come join the play!

A breeze whispers jokes, tickles my ear,
The sun beams laughter, brings good cheer.
With every giggle, the world spins fast,
In this cheerful dance, let's raise a glass!

So raise your voice, let your humor soar,
In nature's circus, we're built for more.
From dawn till dusk, joy is our quest,
Life's better lived with a chuckle and jest!

The Spell of Daytime Light

When morning breaks, the dance begins,
With melted pancakes and syrup wins.
A cat in shades, with sunglasses cool,
Struts like a boss, oh, what a fool!

The sun throws darts of golden rays,
Tickling our cheeks in mischievous ways.
A dog chases shadows, slipping and sliding,
As kids make sandcastles, giggles colliding!

Lemonade stands, bright as a cheer,
A bee wearing shades, buzzing near.
With ice cream drips and splashes of fun,
We laugh 'til we're told it's time to run!

So let's embrace this silly delight,
With every chuckle, the heart feels light.
Caught in this spell, let's frolic and play,
For laughter shall rule our sunlit day!

Jubilee of Golden Days

The sun's a jester, playing its part,
As flip-flops squeak with every heart.
Picnics of joy on a checkered sheet,
Watch ants march by, oh, aren't they neat?

With ice cream cones that melt so fast,
Splat! A joke, that's a sticky blast!
Friends roll on grass, it's a tumble fest,
In nature's jubilee, we surely feel blessed!

Bright balloons float, dancing so free,
While a dog named Max plays hide and seek.
Laughter echoes with every cheer,
In our golden days, the joy is clear!

So raise your hands for this silly show,
With smiles like sunshine, let all hearts glow.
In this carnival of laughter and play,
We'll cherish these moments come what may!

Melodies in the Sunlight

The sun sings sweet, a charming tune,
As laughter tumbles like a cartoon.
The grass is a stage for giddy feet,
While ants form lines—oh, what a feat!

A toddler giggles, slips on a slide,
As ice cream surprises from every side.
Frisbees fly high, the giggles increase,
Nature's orchestra plays, and we feast!

A parrot cackles from a nearby tree,
Tell me your secrets, oh wise birdie!
While picnickers munch on homemade pie,
A squirrel steals crumbs, quick as a spy!

So join the chorus of whimsical cheer,
With each sunny note, let's persevere.
In melodies bright, our spirits align,
In this joyous symphony, we all shall shine!

A Hug from Above

A giant orb rolls in the sky,
It shines on me with a wink and a sigh.
I wear my shades, feeling quite cool,
Melted ice cream, drips, oh what a duel!

Fluffy clouds dance like silly sheep,
While I try to take a brisk, sunny leap.
Birds are laughing, can you hear?
Even squirrels laugh, what a delightful cheer!

Flip-flops squeak, a joyful sound,
The sun's warm glow spreads all around.
I trip on sand, oh what a blast,
Laughter echoes, time flies so fast!

So here I am, with a silly grin,
Chasing shadows, don't know where to begin.
In the sun's embrace, we run and play,
Finding joy in the silliest way!

The Lustrous Horizon

A gleaming ball of orange delight,
It peeks and giggles at the end of the night.
The horizon's joke never gets old,
Each sunset a story, waiting to be told.

Sunbeams tickle, as they creep,
Waking flowers from their sleepy heap.
The trees join in, sway with glee,
Their branches wave, 'Come dance with me!'

A kite flies high, a colorful spree,
Chasing clouds like it's playing tag, whee!
The warm breeze whispers, tales of the day,
While I stumble, as if in ballet play.

With laughter echoing through the air,
I sip cold drinks without a care.
The horizon smiles, a golden crown,
In this land of giggles, I'll never frown!

The Sweetness of Sunny Hours

Lemonade stands and giggles loud,
Kids hop around, oh so proud.
Melting popsicles drip like a joke,
Sugar rush makes us bounce, provoke!

Picnic blankets in the grass,
Sandwiches vanish, oh what a pass.
Here comes a bee, wearing a frown,
Buzzing loudly, time to sit down!

Splashing water, a playful fight,
Sun-kissed faces, everyone's a sight.
Flip a coin, heads or tails?
Under bright skies, our laughter prevails!

Chasing shadows in a playful race,
With silly smiles on every face.
Sweet moments wrapped in giggles and cheer,
Each sunny hour brings friends near!

Glorious Days of Laughter

A day so bright, laughter in the air,
Sunshine tickling without a care.
Ice cream sprinkles, silly and bold,
Every cone a prank waiting to unfold.

Laughing at clouds that look like cows,
In this radiant realm, we take our bows.
Jumping puddles, oops, splashed a shoe,
But who can worry? We've all been through!

Sunglasses perched, like a cool cat,
We strut around, having a chat.
The sun takes selfies, shining so bright,
Memories captured, oh what a sight!

With every giggle under the beam,
Life takes on a whimsical theme.
Glorious days where joy takes flight,
In the sun's embrace, everything's right!

Beneath Golden Rays

We run with shadows, toes in sand,
Chasing ice cream that slips from hand.
The seagulls caw, they join our race,
Muffin crumbs strewn, we'll leave no trace.

A beach ball bounces, high and wide,
Splashing in waves, we take a ride.
With laughter loud, we tumble and roll,
Sunburned noses, oh, that's our goal.

Dancing with Sunlight

We twirl like dervishes on green grass,
Straw hats askew, oh, what a classy pass!
Tickled by rays, we prance and leap,
While neighbors peer, their chuckles deep.

Socks and sandals, we wear with flair,
Feigning elegance, who can compare?
Our every step, a comical sight,
Dancing with sunlight, pure delight.

Embracing Daybreak's Glow

With pancakes flipping, we greet the morn,
Syrup rivers flood the table, oh, so worn!
Spill a little, watch it slide,
A sticky hug we'll never hide.

Sun beams beam through dripping trees,
Telling tales in a warm, sweet breeze.
Birds join in, sing out a tune,
While we juggle breakfast, fork and spoon.

Warmth That Kisses the Skin

A sunlit picnic, laughter in the air,
Sunscreen smeared, we are without a care.
Sandwiches fly as we tell our jokes,
With ants in a line, now that's the hoax!

A frisbee swoops, a daring chase,
Oops, it lands on a snoozy face!
With giggles burst, we all take flight,
Under blue skies, we bask in light.

The Jewel of Daylight

Golden beams make shadows dance,
While squirrels plot their nutty chance.
The daisies giggle, stretch and yawn,
In this bright game, come one, come dawn.

I saw a crow wearing a hat,
He cawed at me, he looked quite fat.
The sun, a giant glowing coin,
Brings out the humor in this join.

Picnics full of spills and thrills,
Jumping kids and rolling hills.
The ants march in their tiny squads,
Conducting feasts for hungry gods.

So grab your shades, let laughter reign,
In daylight's bright and funny lane.
For every smile that we can spread,
Is like a sunshine sandwich spread.

Heaven's Hue

Bright colors burst like bubble gum,
As clouds play dress-up, oh so fun!
With every sunbeam's cheeky poke,
Yeah, pigeons crack the silliest joke.

The flowers wear their brightest attire,
While bees zoom by like they're on fire.
A cat in shades just takes a nap,
Dreaming of fish, perhaps a wrap.

The laughter echoes through the trees,
As nature dances with the breeze.
Tickling toes on grassy floors,
With goofy moves, we open doors.

So let the sky be our delight,
With silly moments, hearts take flight.
For in this joy, come laugh along,
In every shade where we belong.

Flickers of Joy on Warm Winds

Breezes tickle as they play,
While butterflies weave bright ballet.
A dog chases its wagging tail,
And ice cream drips, oh what a trail!

Children chase the fading sun,
With laughter shared, oh what fun!
A kite gets stuck upon a tree,
Awkward giggles, can't you see?

The hammock sways with a goofy grin,
While spiders spin their webs so thin.
As clouds pass by like fluffy sheep,
In warm embrace, no worries, sleep.

So raise a toast to silliness,
With every laugh, we feel the bliss.
For in these moments, fun will spark,
Like fireflies dancing in the dark.

Life Illuminated by Radiance

Sunshine spills on sidewalks bright,
Chasing shadows, what a sight!
The world is dressed in yellow cheer,
Inviting giggles, loud and near.

A cat on a fence with majestic flair,
Pretends to conduct a solar fair.
While birds burst into song and jest,
Nature's stand-up, surely the best!

Laughter echoes in the air,
As friends attach a silly dare.
Through radiant days, our hearts align,
Painting joy with laughter's sign.

So let the glow of light bestow,
A pathway where our chuckles flow.
In every beam that breaks the night,
We'll dance together, pure delight.

The Embrace of Heat and Light

The sun gave my ice cream a wink,
Melting away faster than I could think.
My hat flew off, a kite in the air,
I chased it down like a summer fair!

Sizzling sidewalks, shoes felt like glue,
A puddle danced, trying to woo.
With sweat on my brow, I'd make a toast,
To the sun's hot embrace and the tan I boast!

Sunbeams and Shadows

Sunbeams tickle, a playful tease,
Shadows stretch out, seeking some breeze.
A squirrel stole my sandwich with glee,
While laughter bubbled from the old oak tree.

In sunglasses bold, I strut down the lane,
Pretending I'm famous, avoiding the rain.
The sun's on my side, giving me flair,
While birds serenade without a care!

When Light Meets Earth

The light grins down, it's not shy at all,
Grass tickles my feet, I feel small.
A frisbee returns like a confused boomerang,
While dogs bark at shadows, it's all quite the clang!

Lemonade stands pop up with a cheer,
Kids barter for ice with a charm not so clear.
With sunflowers tall, I must say with delight,
They're swaying to music, what a funny sight!

Reveling in Day's Embrace

Picnic blankets spread like a patchwork quilt,
Sandwiches squashed, and juice spilled.
Laughter erupts as the ants march on,
Stealing crumbs while we're plotting a con.

Chasing the rays as the clouds float by,
A burp escapes, and we all laugh and sigh.
This silliness glows amidst green and gold,
With the sun beaming down, our stories unfold!

The Dance of Sunbeams

When rays of light begin to bounce,
The flowers start their happy flounce.
A squirrel twirls, a bird will prance,
In nature's silly, sunny dance.

The grasses sway, they twist and twirl,
A ladybug dons her best pearl.
With every step, the shadows play,
As sunbeams join the wild ballet.

A cat sprawls out, he basks in pride,
While laughter rolls like a joyful tide.
The bees buzz low, they're feeling grand,
In brightened fields, all mischief planned.

From every nook, the giggles rise,
The sun spills joy like birthday pies.
With silly hats and laughter sound,
The daylight party spins around.

Bright Horizons Rising

A rooster crows, the sun takes cue,
And what a sight, the world anew.
The shadows stretch, they yawn so wide,
While silly clouds begin to glide.

The pancakes flip, they dance on plates,
With syrup rivers that love their mates.
A tiny ant in grand parade,
Invites his friends, "Don't be afraid!"

The morning laughter fills the air,
As sunshine spills without a care.
The toast does a little jig and sway,
In a brightened world where fun holds sway.

With every splash and giggly cheer,
The day ahead brings nothing near.
No frowns allowed in this delight,
Just silly smiles from morning light.

Sunlit Whispers of Dawn

When morning yawns and winks at me,
A butterfly flaps, "Come dance with thee!"
The grass is fresh, as if it drank,
A bubbly drink from nature's tank.

A kitten peeks from shade to sun,
His whiskers twitch, "Let's have some fun!"
The dew drops cheer with tiny spark,
As roly-polies start their arc.

A laugh resounds from every peep,
While little creatures wake from sleep.
With sunshine's glow, the giggles soar,
As nature whispers, "Let's explore!"

The world is bright, the day is free,
With dancing leaves and buzzing glee.
With every step, let joy thus roam,
In sunlit fields, we've found our home.

The Magic of Midday Light

We roam beneath the wide blue sky,
As clouds put on their fluffy tie.
The sun beams down with such a grin,
While bugs all bust their best chagrin.

A picnic rug is spread with cheer,
Where ants parade and sip their beer.
The lemonade spills from the cup,
As giggles burst, "Let's mix it up!"

The ice cream drips down every cone,
A sticky treat, but never alone.
We race the breeze, we leap and shout,
Waves of laughter dance about.

With every splash and silly game,
We write our stories, none the same.
For in this glowing, cheerful sight,
We find the joy — a sheer delight!

Blushing Petals in Daylight

Petals blush as they soak,
Daisies giggle, that's no joke.
Butterflies dance, play hide and seek,
In bright hues, they peek and squeak.

Bees wear snooze caps, buzzing by,
Waving their tiny wings to fly.
Lemonade spills, laughter erupts,
Sweet summer antics, who interrupts?

Gardens sport a riot of glee,
Sun hats flying, oh, what a spree!
Worms throw parties under the ground,
While squirrels make mischief all around.

The sun throws confetti all day long,
Chasing shadows, a cheery song.
In this carnival where whimsy glows,
Nature laughs, the fun just grows!

Sunlit Reveries

Frogs wear shades on lily pads,
Giggling loudly, oh, how they've mad.
Ducks have disco moves, so slick,
Twirling in water, oh, what a trick!

Sunbeam selfies, a radiant chat,
With daisies wearing their finest hat.
Clouds drift by, making faces,
Hide and seek in their fluffy paces.

Squirrels host races, tails all a'flick,
Racing to acorns, quick, quick, quick!
Ants line dance, one, two, three,
Grooving to nature's jubilee.

As laughter weaves through the warm air,
Every creature has a tale to share.
In this land of sunshine's fun,
Joy blooms brightly, we all run!

Elysian Fields Awash in Gold

Fields twinkle like jewels in light,
Hopping hare jokes, such a delight.
Winking wildflowers, oh so spry,
While butterflies pirouette up high.

The grass tickles toes running past,
Chasing clouds, not a thought to cast.
Crickets make beats, a summer throng,
Nature's concert, where all belong.

Fluffy sheep wear smiles and cheer,
Their woolly jokes bring laughter near.
Caterpillars strut in style so bold,
With dreams of wings, their hearts unfold.

In this golden glow of mirth,
Every moment's a fresh rebirth.
With laughter dancing on gentle breeze,
Joy spreads wide, as we all seize!

Illuminated Hearts

Children's giggles bounce off walls,
Bubbles rising, oh, the joy enthralls.
Ice cream drips, a sweet sticky mess,
Laughter erupts; it's nothing but zest!

Silly hats parade on heads so fine,
With flowers, feathers, truly divine.
Chasing shadows, a fab charade,
In bright revelry, memories made.

Birds perform a comical show,
Singing tunes with a cheeky glow.
Sun's warm touch on cheeks so bright,
Every heart dances in pure light.

As nightfall whispers, joy won't cease,
In our dreams, we find sweet peace.
With laughter echoing through the lanes,
In this cheerful place, love reigns!

The Lullaby of Sunlit Dreams

In a hammock slung so low,
A squirrel steals my nacho show.
The sunbeams dance upon my face,
While ants hold their wacky race.

My drink's a puddle, oh what glee,
A cat's decided it's for she.
The lemonade's become a lake,
As ducks plan their little break.

I lounge while my cares drift away,
The seagulls plot their loud buffet.
Hot dogs sizzle, it's quite absurd,
My napkin's now a nest for birds.

With giggles from kids, laughter swells,
A sunburn friend's a funny tale to tell.
With shades as big as saucers, oh dear,
I'm the star of this sunny frontier.

Radiance on the Horizon

A beach ball bounces, oh what fun,
It knocks a sandwich from my bun.
The waves are laughing, it seems absurd,
As I chase seagulls, not a single word.

Bikini tops sail in salty breeze,
While sunscreen flies like bees to trees.
I trip on flip-flops, fall, then roll,
As sunburned friends become the goal.

Ice cream drips down my weary hand,
As kids play tag across the sand.
A sunhat flies, a wild chase,
While I just giggle, red-faced in place.

The sun sets low, the day's a gem,
And now I'm wearing someone's hem.
With laughter echoing, night begins,
A silly dance, where no one wins.

Sunlit Whispers in the Breeze

On a picnic blanket, wobbly and bright,
I reach for a sandwich, it takes flight.
The ants are now the true gourmet,
As all my snacks just run away.

Bubbles float on the golden rays,
While a child misspells "sunny" in plays.
A giggling dog has found my hat,
And prances away – imagine that!

A lemonade stand draws all the kids,
But I'm just standing, feeling like lids.
Watermelons squirt like playful foes,
And my laughter, goodness, it just grows.

As fireflies blink in evening's nudge,
I spot a cat who won't budge.
With funny tales woven through the night,
Our joyful hearts take playful flight.

Gilded Moments at Dusk

The evening sky is cotton candy,
While a frog hops like it's quite dandy.
The laughter spills like soda pop,
As we dance around, no need to stop.

A frisbee thwacks my sister's head,
But she just giggles, "I'm not dead!"
The sunset hues give all a glow,
While fireflies shimmy, putting on a show.

A loud "oops" as I spill my drink,
And everyone pauses just to think.
Tonight's the night for funny blunders,
As twilight whispers soft, in wonder.

The stars emerge, the moon pulls tight,
While we chase shadows in the light.
With friendship wrapped in evening's charm,
This funny dawn feels like a balm.

Threads of Gold in the Air

Bees buzz like tiny jets,\
Chasing flowers with no regrets,\
Ants throw a picnic parade,\
While sunbeams dance in a charade.\
\
Butterflies wear polka-dot gowns,\
As squirrels play tag with sleeping crowns,\
The breeze hums tunes of playful lore,\
While we grumble 'Why is life a chore?'\
\
Grass tickles toes; oh what a prank,\
As laughter echoes down the plank,\
In a world where shadows take a nap,\
And sun-soaked joy forms a bright map.\
\
The day slips by, slipping like goo,\
With every slip, we find something new,\
Chasing shadows, rolling in glee,\
Wishing moments would float like the bee.

Awakening the Senses in Sunshine

The toast pops up like a clown's nose,\
As orange juice dances and flows,\
Pancakes stack, a syrupy tower,\
And breakfast blooms like a sweet flower.\
\
Birds belt out a coffee shop tune,\
While socks play hide and seek at noon,\
A sunbeam tickles the cat's chin,\
And suddenly, the day can begin.\
\
With lemonade spills and ice cream drips,\
We shape our fun with silly quips,\
Jumps and giggles fill the air,\
Here's to days without a care!\
\
Wrap it up in laughter bright,\
Chase the shadows; wayward flight,\
With every color ripe and bold,\
We paint our days with threads of gold.

Illuminating Nature's Palette

Clouds fluff up like cotton candy,\
And daisies giggle as they stand handy,\
Sticks become swords in a wild fight,\
As the sun paints each moment bright.\
\
A tree teases the swing with a grin,\
While sticks and stones join the din,\
With every shadow, silly tricks play,\
And laughter stretches the hours away.\
\
Sunflowers sport hats with flair,\
And frogs leap with no sense of care,\
The squirrels hold a tea party spree,\
While bees form a band, dancing for free!\
\
Each color shines, vibrant and loud,\
Nature laughs, a bright and zany crowd,\
In a symphony of joyful cheer,\
We embrace the fun that's always near.

Embracing Summer's Bounty

Berries burst like tiny fireworks,\
As pickers play tag with little quirks,\
The corn on the cob grins wide in rows,\
While tomatoes blush from their garden pose.\
\
Chasing chickens, we skip and run,\
Racing shadows, oh what fun,\
With juice on our faces, a sticky show,\
As laughter floats like fireflies' glow.\
\
The hammock sways like a dancer's spin,\
While popsicles melt — oh, what a sin!\
Lemonade stands with giddy charm,\
We toast to the sun, raising the farm.\
\
And when twilight wraps us in gold,\
We share the stories bright and bold,\
In fields of laughter, hearts are free,\
Embracing the joy that summer can be.

A Canvas of Light

The sky is a painter, bright and bold,
With splashes of yellow and hints of gold.
Squirrels wear shades, strutting all day,
While sunflowers giggle, in their own sway.

The bird on the branch, tunes up his song,
Complaining about the sunbeams too strong.
A lizard takes selfies, by the warm rock,
Laughing at shadows that suddenly mock.

Butterflies flutter, on their sweet quest,
Trying to find where they can rest.
The picnic ants march, a line so neat,
Stealing the crumbs of a sandwich treat.

Beneath this brightness, where laughter streams,
We'll dance like fools, in sunbeam dreams.
What a joyous rhythm, life's grand parade,
In a canvas of light, we're all unafraid.

Serenity in the Rays

Beneath a glow that feels just right,
We find the peace that shines so bright.
A cat in a sunbeam, takes a grand pose,
Dreaming of fish, or so it goes.

The grass is a trampoline, everyone's game,
While bees take turns, in a dance that's the same.
They buzz and they bop, with style and glee,
Making a ruckus in their own honoree.

The blanket is spread, snacks galore,
But the ants hold a meeting, planning to score.
A slice of watermelon, oh what a treat,
But watch your slice, they're quick on their feet.

In rays of joy, the world is a jest,
We laugh at the antics, feeling so blessed.
In this sunny realm, all quirks are okay,
Serenity blooms in the light of the day.

Laughter in the Afternoon Glow

In the afternoon glow, silliness reigns,
As children play tag, ignoring all pains.
A dog chases shadows with floppy delight,
While nearby a frog, jumps to take flight.

The ice cream truck sings a catchy refrain,
But melted cones lead to hilarious pain.
Watch out for sprinkles, like confetti they fly,
More on your shirt than in your pie.

A kite takes a dive, with a wild swoop,
And the crowd erupts in a chuckling loop.
The sun plays tag with the clouds on the run,
Each peek-a-boo moment, a barrel of fun.

As laughter takes over, and skies turn pink,
We share all our secrets, and no one will blink.
In this humorous haven, with echoes so loud,
We find joy in laughter, and life is unbowed.

The Warmth of a Brilliant Embrace

A round of applause for the sun's funny face,
It tickles the flowers, oh what a place!
The clouds wear sombreros, quite out of style,
Cheering up dull days, making us smile.

We lounge like sloths, in the golden embrace,
While bugs gather round for a grand tasting race.
A grasshopper challenges, with hops that amaze,
While bees throw a party, in swirling arrays.

A picnic is hapless, with ants galore,
Stealing the crumbs, demanding for more.
A mishap with lemonade, sticky and sweet,
Turns laughter to bubbles, a fizzy treat!

In this warmth, we unite, no shadow of frown,
Collecting the giggles, never let down.
Life's a grand stage, with roles all aglow,
In the embrace of this brilliance, we joyfully flow.

Memories in the Sunshine

Lemonade spills, laughter flies,
Chasing shadows as time sighs.
A sunburnt nose, a silly dance,
In golden hues, we take our chance.

Picnic crumbs on giggling toes,
As daisies bloom in silly rows.
We juggle dreams with ice cream cones,
Life's a joke, let's share the phones.

Sun hats worn in joyful grace,
Silly selfies, that goofy face.
The day drips sweet with radiant cheer,
Let's make memories that last all year.

With every laugh, the sunbeam blinks,
In this light, the world winks.
We dance like dandelions afloat,
Each moment a tickle, a funny note.

Emptiness Filled with Light

Socks mismatched, a sunny glee,
Chasing clouds like wild bees.
With every slip, a burst of cheer,
In this madness, we hold dear.

A picnic spread, we feast on air,
With invisible pies, we share a stare.
The warmth envelops our thoughts so bright,
As laughter echoes, taking flight.

Wobbly chairs on a sunlit deck,
We dance like puppets, what the heck?
The world feels light, absurdly bright,
As we twirl in joy, hearts take flight.

An empty cup, a remnant swirl,
We toast to nothing, let laughter twirl.
In brightness found, a jester's delight,
Our hearts grow bold, chasing the light.

The Luminous World Around

Butterflies wearing tiny shoes,
In this bright land, we chase the blues.
Sunshine tickles the trees so high,
With giggling squirrels tapping by.

A grass-stained shirt, oh what a sight,
We roll and tumble in sheer delight.
The golden rays wrap us in a hug,
As we bounce like balls, wild and snug.

With laughter loud, we skip and weave,
The luminous world makes us believe.
Every shadow dances with flair,
In this magical, radiant air.

Bubbles float, like bubbles of glee,
As cotton candy clouds hug the sea.
We sing with joy, in the bright expanse,
Join hands and spin, let's take a chance.

Glowing Dreams in Bloom

A garden of giggles, flowers sway,
In wobbly shades, we find our play.
Silly hats on absurd grand schemes,
In this place, we chase our dreams.

With butterflies laughing, we jump around,
Each little moment, joyfully found.
Sun-kissed cheeks, in this light we bloom,
Our laughter echoes, filling the room.

Dandelion wishes take off in flight,
As we dream silly 'til the stars ignite.
With every chuckle, the petals sing,
In a world of shining, let's take wing.

A dance of sunshine, twirls and spins,
In every giggle, a playful grin.
Through glowing fields, we march in tune,
Chasing our dreams beneath the moon.

Rays of Joy and Laughter

Sunshine tickles my cheek,
And the birds all let out a squeak.
I dance like no one's around,
As squirrels laugh and roll on the ground.

Crickets sing with such zest,
While I try my very best.
To catch rays in my cup,
But they just giggle and leap up.

A dog joins my merry spree,
Chasing shadows just like me.
We roll in the grass so green,
Living life like a fun-filled dream.

So come join the joyful ride,
Where laughter and light collide.
With every chuckle in the air,
We share this warmth everywhere!

Beneath Golden Skies

With a hat too big for my head,
And ice cream melting instead.
I chase after dreams and bees,
While looking for shade under trees.

A butterfly flaps with glee,
Teasing me, can't you see?
I trip over my own two feet,
And land in flowers, oh so sweet!

Clouds above all fluff and pink,
I ponder what I should drink.
A smoothie? A soda pop?
Or I might just take a flop!

Laughing at bees with no care,
I spin in circles, oh so rare.
Joy bubbles like soda pop,
With every giggle, I can't stop!

Embracing Daylight's Glow

Hot dogs grilling in the sun,
Who knew they'd be so much fun?
I flip one high, it lands with a flop,
And dogs below just can't stop!

A frisbee soars, but oh, what a mess,
It lands on my friend's sundress.
A picnic blanket waves in a breeze,
As ants march with such expertise!

With lemonade splashes all around,
We create the silliest sound.
I wear my drink like a new scarf,
While everyone bursts into laughter's half.

The sun sets down but we won't go,
Chasing laughter, stealing the show.
A day well spent with friends so dear,
In this glow, we have no fear!

Radiance on a Quiet Meadow

Middle of nowhere, what a treat,
I lie back on warm, soft wheat.
A ladybug starts to sway,
As if to groove and play!

The grass tickles my toes,
While I strike a pose, who knows?
A goat peeks over the hill,
Winking at me, what a thrill!

Suddenly a cloud forms a hat,
And I giggle, imagine that!
The sun shines bright with a grin,
As if it knows we'll begin to spin!

So here's to the joy that we chase,
Finding laughter in every space.
In meadows, beneath the big sky,
We'll burst out loud and never be shy!

Time Paused in Solstice Light

When the clocks all seem to melt,
And my pencil starts to wilt.
I toss my worries in the breeze,
As ants run off with my cheese.

The dog wears shades, looks so cool,
He drags me back, acts like a fool.
Squirrels play tag on the lawn,
They giggle, 'Oh, come on, come on!'

A sunbeam dances on my head,
Turns my toast into burnt bread.
Butterflies chase after a fly,
While I'm busy just asking why.

Lemonade spills down my shirt,
"Was that a sip or is it dessert?"
The sun laughs loud, it's quite a scene,
With shades and smiles; what a routine!

A Moment of Celestial Glow

The sun spills gold across my lawn,
As I stumble, trip, and yawn.
A flock of birds sings out of tune,
While I dance like a baboon.

My hat flies off, it claims the air,
A frisbee lands—was that a dare?
Grass stains now cover my knee,
But I look awesome, can't you see?

A cat in shades gives me a wink,
As I recline, starting to sink.
The sky whispers secrets to the tree,
"Can I borrow some shade?" says me.

The world's a circus in this light,
While I juggle laughter, what a sight!
With every giggle, I lose my mind,
Yet in this chaos, joy I find!

The Symphony of Bright Rays

Sunlight strums the roof so bright,
Birds conduct with pure delight.
I play the air guitar like mad,
Neighbors frown, but I'm so glad.

The breeze is a cheeky little sprite,
Tickling the flowers, oh what a sight!
My sandwich flies; it takes a stand,
While ants form a marching band.

The sun plays peek-a-boo with my hat,
As my dog chases a hapless cat.
I shout a tune, I dance, I spin,
While time invites me to join in.

So we all waltz in rays so sweet,
With ticklish grass beneath our feet.
In this symphony of every laugh,
I find a silly photograph!

The Enchantment of Daylight

A sunbeam's hug feels warm and tight,
As shadows morph to silly sight.
A gopher pokes his head up high,
He's confused—"Am I a spy?"

I chase my hat down the lane,
While all the bees buzz at my brain.
Butterflies beg for a selfie pose,
"Oooh, I'm fabulous!" everyone knows.

The sun throws a party for the trees,
While I try not to trip on my knees.
Dandelion wishes sail through the sky,
And I wonder why I can't fly.

As giggles echo through warm air,
I take a moment to just stare.
In this enchantment, laughter's the key,
So come dance with joy, madcap and free!

Fields Bathed in Brilliance

Grass tickles my toes, oh what a tease,
A butterfly lands, just trying to please.
Bees buzzing around, they're quite the loud crew,
While I sip lemonade, not a worry in view.

Sunflowers dance, all dressed up in gold,
Their cheerful faces, a sight to behold.
A tumbleweed rolls, with a laugh it does twirl,
Trying to join in, oh what a strange whirl!

The sky wears a smile, it's cheering with glee,
While I try to catch jellybeans falling from trees.
A squirrel steals my snack, with a mischievous grin,
I chase him on foot, but he's quick as the wind!

With warmth all around, I'll dance like a fool,
In this land of delight, it's the best kind of school.
Let's frolic and giggle, like kids in the park,
Where sunshine's a friend, and joy leaves a mark.

Glimmers of an Endless Summer

A lazy cat naps on a warm patch of light,
While I chase my dreams, like a kite in flight.
The ice cream melts fast, drips down to my toes,
I laugh at the mess, improvising some prose.

A picnic spread out, ants join in the fun,
Sharing my sandwich? Well, that's a bold run.
The seagulls are cackling, they think they're so sly,
They dive for my fries, oh my, oh my!

The days stretch on, like a slinky that bends,
I giggle with friends, we're all making amends.
Our laughter rings out, like bells in the breeze,
Two suntanned toes waved, oh what a tease!

A hammock sways gently, I take a quick rest,
Yet a featherweight pillow steals all my zest.
I dream of pie fights, with whipped cream galore,
Waking up with sprinkles? I couldn't ask for more!

Caressed by the Light

The sun's golden beams tickle my face,
I sprint in delight, like a wild, silly race.
Flip-flops are flopping, on this hot sandy turf,
And I trip over shells, what a comical surf!

My friend says, 'Look, a cloud shaped like cheese!'
We giggle and snort like it's sure to please.
Frolicking seagulls dive, stealing our snacks,
We wave our arms wildly, like crazy hijacks!

Splashes and giggles, water fights often,
The sun plays my DJ, my worries are lost in.
I pretend to be mermaid, in this crystal clear sea,
While my sunscreen quest becomes quite the spree!

But oh, what's this? A crab with a strut,
Marching like royalty, not caring a nut.
He steals my last chip, with one click of his claws,
While I chuckle and chase, letting out loud guffaws.

Sun-kissed Dreams

My hat flies away, like a bird on a spree,
Chasing its shadow, oh how funny can be!
As I dash down the street, the sun waves goodbye,
It's a race with the wind, as I giggle and fly.

Flip-flops go flapping, I'm rhythmically bold,
With a grin of delight, letting my joy unfold.
Bubbles are floating, a rainbow parade,
I pop them with laughter, my worries all fade.

The garden's alive, with the craziest sounds,
Rabbits are dancing in their little round bounds.
A snail slides by slow, offers a grin,
And I whisper, "Hey buddy, let's look for some gin!"

The evening arrives, sparkles fill up the skies,
We toast with our sodas, and watch the sun's rise.
Dreams all around, as we laugh 'til we fall,
Living life silly, I'll cherish it all!

Radiant Footsteps on Warm Sand

Sandy toes, they dance around,
A crab scuttles, he's quite profound.
I trip and tumble, laugh with glee,
The sun thinks it's a comedy spree.

Seagulls giggle at my silly hats,
While sunburns form in funny spats.
I slather lotion, yet I shine,
Like a lobster? Oh, that's just fine!

Footprints lead to nowhere fast,
Chasing waves like it's a blast.
The ocean giggles, splashes near,
Calling me a silly seer.

In playful tides, I lose my shoe,
The sun just laughs, it knows it's true.
With sandy friends and giggles grand,
Life's a jest, all unplanned.

An Afternoon's Gentle Flame

A blanket spread beneath the rays,
We snack on snacks that never pays.
I spilled my juice, it's on my face,
The ants will have a lovely race.

Lemonade spills, oh what a sight!
I toast the sun, it's just too bright.
My shades fall off, I squint and grin,
That's my life, let the fun begin!

A frisbee flies, it's not so sleek,
It lands on Grandma's picnic leak.
She fakes a gasp, but has a laugh,
I dodge the mishap, take my path.

The sun begins to chase the shade,
We swap our chairs, a sunny trade.
Lively tales and laughter soar,
The day's bright spirit, we adore.

The Glow of Golden Moments

The pancakes flip, they catch the light,
Syrup splashes, oh what a sight!
Butter melts just a tad too quick,
I'm a chef? Maybe not, that's the trick.

The garden blooms in colors bright,
I chase the dog, we're quite a sight.
He trips on toys, a comic flop,
The flowers giggle as they bop!

Sunshine drips from every seam,
As butterflies flit, it's like a dream.
I dance with shadows, feet in play,
Joy in motion, what can I say?

The golden hour whispers tales,
Of silly pranks and wind-swept sails.
We bask in hope, in laughter's glow,
In this bright world, together we grow.

Sunlit Pathways

Wandering paths in sandals worn,
A flip-flop saga, I was sworn.
To dodge the puddles with a breeze,
I end up drenched, but still I tease.

The trees are laughing, what a crew,
Their branches wave, they mock me too.
I run, I skip, I trip on roots,
And giggle loud as nature hoots.

In every step, a joy parade,
A dancing squirrel, a wild charade.
The sun plays hide and seek with clouds,
While I'm the team's most goofy louds.

A picnic planned, but ants on guard,
I share my lunch, it's not that hard.
With shades on, we unite and cheer,
In sunlit pathways, laughter's near.

A Serenade of Sunlight

Golden beams bounce off my head,
A hat too small, I'm seeing red.
Chasing shadows in a race,
My sunburnt nose, a funny face.

Birds are chirping, quite the show,
Dancing squirrels put on a glow.
I trip on grass, oh what a fall,
A giggle erupts, I can't stand tall.

Ice cream drips down on my shirt,
Melting faster, oh the hurt!
Sticky fingers, can't shake it off,
I laugh aloud, a joyful scoff.

Sunset hints, day's almost done,
Counting laughs, oh what fun!
Tomorrow brings the shining beams,
With friends, we'll dance and chase our dreams.

Nature's Caress

Daisies tickle, grass is high,
I'm convinced the clouds can fly.
A playful breeze, it pulls my hair,
I twist and twirl, without a care.

Chasing butterflies in a dart,
They laugh and tease without a heart.
A frog jumps in, what a splash!
I stumble back, oh what a crash!

Lemonade spills, oh what a mess,
Sticky sweetness, who would guess?
The ants march on, they seem so proud,
I can't help laughing, way too loud!

As the sun begins to fade,
I daydream under the glade.
With laughter echoing, time flies fast,
In nature's hands, my heart is cast.

Rays of Hope

The sun peeks through, a cheeky grin,
A race begins; let's see who'll win!
With towels flying, we take our stand,
But who will land in the sand?

Jumping waves, the splashes soar,
I flounder back, but want to explore.
My friend's hat flies, a wild sight,
Chasing it 'til it's out of sight!

Caught a glimpse of jellyfish,
A wobbling friend, the strangest wish.
I poke it gently, it jiggles back,
With giggles shared, we've got no lack.

But as day ends, I must confess,
Sunshine's fun can be a mess.
Still, every ray brings laughter bright,
In its warm glow, all feels right.

The Splendor of Brightness

Dancing rays, a goofy dance,
We twirl and spin, oh what a chance!
With silly faces, the sunlight beams,
Who cares 'bout plans? Let's chase our dreams!

A picnic spread on grass so green,
Muffins rolling, what a scene!
I reach for fruit, but oh dear me,
The ants get there first, they're quick, you see!

Sun hats worn at silly angles,
Giving off vibes that make them dangle.
My friend sneezes, a feathered hat,
Flying high—what's up with that?

As laughter bubbles like a stream,
Every moment feels like a dream.
Chasing sunsets, with all my crew,
Each warm day is hilariously new!

Shimmering Reflections

In a pond where ducks float by,
Swaying hats are lost with a sigh.
A frog croaks jokes to a curious fish,
While sunbeams dance, granting each wish.

The turtles sunbathe with such style,
One fell asleep, dreaming a while.
A dragonfly buzzed, couldn't stand still,
While ants held a parade, quite the thrill!

Bubbles rise with each laughter burst,
The cat pounced in, sparking a first.
Fish wore sunglasses - oh what a sight!
Water fights began, what a delight!

With splashes and giggles, they all convene,
A riot of fun, a happy routine.
As the day winds down in a playful hush,
Reflections shimmer, the world in a rush.

Dappled Sunshine in the Glade

In the glade where the fireflies dance,
Squirrels prance, take a chance!
A raccoon with shades, oh what a scene,
He's the coolest critter you've ever seen!

Grasshoppers sing in a jazzy fight,
While bunnies enforce a hop-hop delight.
A tall tree with branches so wide,
Gives out free shade, come and abide!

The mushrooms are hosting a tea party fair,
With crumpets and jam, oh what a flare!
A snail takes a seat, oh so slow,
His friends all cheer, 'Let's start the show!'

As the sun starts to dip, all gather 'round,
With stories and laughter, joy is found.
In this forest where fun meets the light,
Every creature is dancing through the night.

Warm Embraces of the Sky

The blue above, a canvas so bright,
Clouds become shapes, a peculiar sight.
A bear floats by on a fluffy white,
Waving to kids who grin with delight!

A kite in the breeze is caught in a spin,
While a dog chases shadows, let the fun begin!
Picnics abound on the green grass spread,
As ants steal crumbs, there's laughter instead!

A sunbeam tickles a girl's curly hair,
Her giggles are music, a joyous flare.
With lemonade served from jugs so tall,
Each sip is a splash, a summer ball!

As day turns dusk with a fiery blush,
Everyone's smiling, what a sweet rush!
In the warmth of this playful spree,
The sky meets the laughter, wild and free.

Dreams Wrapped in Light

At twilight's edge, where wishes gleam,
Fireflies flicker, a whimsical dream.
A bear wears pajamas, what a sight to see,
As it dances a jig by the old oak tree!

The stars are winking, sharing their tales,
While the moon grins wide, sailing in gales.
A raccoon reads aloud from a comic book,
While owls roll their eyes in a funny hook!

Cotton candy clouds drift in the sky,
With popcorn rain that makes everyone sigh.
A sleepy hedgehog yawns with delight,
As the world wraps up in shimmering light.

With each little laughter, the night comes alive,
Magic surrounds as we play and thrive.
Dreams wrap us close as we hug the night,
This silly adventure feels perfectly right!

Glimmers of Bliss in Every Ray

Tiny ants march in a line,
Carrying crumbs, feeling fine.
The sun's a giant BBQ,
Grilling my thoughts, tender and true.

Squirrels dance in crazy leaps,
While the lazy dogdoze as he sleeps.
Birds chirp jokes, all in a row,
Their punchlines bright as the golden glow.

Children laugh, chasing their dreams,
Ice cream drips, bursting at seams.
All seems right in the light's embrace,
Even the clouds join in the race!

Ticklish breeze gives hair a tussle,
Sun-kissed skin feels like a cuddle.
Mom's lemonade, sweetened with glee,
Best served with a side of funny!

Sunlit Journeys of the Heart

Sunshine paints the world so bright,
Makes even broccoli seem all right.
Excuse my grin as I fumble around,
Stumbling like a clown on the ground.

Our bicycles wobble, tires in fright,
Pedaling fast with all our might.
But wait! A tumble, and off we go,
Rolling like tumbleweeds in a show.

Kites are flying, tangled in trees,
Making squirrels giggle, if you please.
Oh how we laugh, it's pure delight,
As sunlight wraps us in this light.

With a leap, we dance through the park,
Chasing shadows until it's dark.
In every breeze, we find a jest,
Laughter carries us on this quest!

As Daylight Stitches Time

Golden thread weaves through the skies,
Crafting moments, oh what a prize!
Time is fabric, light is the seam,
We run like kids, chasing a dream.

Tick-tock goes the sunny clock,
It makes us dance and do the rock.
Every tick is a giggle and cheer,
With rays that hug us, never fear!

Sun-melted ice cream drips down fast,
Moments like this are made to last.
We laugh at time, what a funny trick,
For it loves to play, a magic flick!

With silly hats and sunglasses bright,
We strut our stuff in pure daylight.
So come, my friend, let's twirl and spin,
As daylight stitches joy within!

The Symphony of Glow

A symphony plays beneath the rays,
As birds compose their cheeky ways.
Grasshopper taps on a leaf so green,
While ants form a band, just unseen.

Sunlight dances, casting long shadows,
Silly shapes make us laugh like hallowed brows.
The breeze hums along with a grin,
As we sway and twirl, letting joy in.

Picnics spread out on checkered cloth,
With sandwiches singing, oh what a troth!
Pickles jive and chips make a mess,
While we laugh loud, who can guess?

The glow of the world keeps the rhythm alive,
With every chuckle, we joyfully thrive.
For in the laughter, the tune we find,
A melody of sunshine's kind!

www.ingramcontent.com/pod-product-compliance
Lightning Source LLC
Chambersburg PA
CBHW072130070526
44585CB00016B/1609